"A JOURNEY OF A THOUSAND

MILES BEGINS WITH A SINGLE

STEP."

Table of Contents:

For more books, please visit the above page or visit our website at innersparkgoods.com

Thank You

Commitment: I understand that I can only succeed through hard work and will take the initiative in my learning. Because I want to succeed as an entrepreneur in online business and, I will apply commitment to the tools, techniques, tips, and strategies shared in this book as the support to my success. I understand that the ultimate responsibility for succeeding is in my control. I 100% commit.

Name (print) _____

Signature_____

Introduction

Embark on Your Ecommerce Adventure

Hey there, future online store owner, Beginning your journey with an online business? Get ready for an exciting ride into the digital world, where you can make money and succeed. But hey, every trip has its difficulties, right? Don't worry, I've got your back and will help you make your own online store.

The goods you sell are the heart of your business. Take some time to think about what makes your goods unique before you get into the technical stuff. Ask yourself: What issues do your goods fix? Why do we need them? Do you think your prices are fair for what you're giving? Just what makes your goods different?

Now comes the fun part, getting your online store set up. Be smart about which site you pick because it could make or break your business. Options like WooCommerce, Shopify, BigCommerce, and Square are not only dependable, but they're also easy for beginners to use. You can make your website look however you want with their help.

Make your website look better by adding great product descriptions, photos, and movies that people will want to watch. Don't forget to offer different ways for customers to pay either. Credit cards, PayPal, and services like Afterpay can make it easy for them to buy from you. Also, having your email connected to Gmail? It changes the game for good conversation.

The next thing we need to talk about is traffic. Learn about the three types: sponsored, held, and acquired. Keep an eye on important data so you can make smart choices. Find out what your bounce and exit rates are and work on raising your conversion rate. You can also use smart strategies to raise the average order value.

Check out Judge.me and other review sites to get customer comments that you can use to build trust. Great customer service is important. A live chat feature on your website can help a lot. Always keep in mind that e-commerce is a world that is always changing. Listen to podcasts, read books, watch videos, and connect with teachers who have been through it all.

Keep learning and being flexible as you go through e-commerce. Most importantly, put your customers first. A successful online store depends on having happy customers. With these things in place, you can start building an online business that does well and grows.

Now, let's talk more about the most important things that will make you stand out in the e-commerce world. These are like your secret tools for getting things done.

Conversion Rate Optimization (CRO): Imagine getting more people who visit your website to buy something. In fact, that's what CRO does. Work on it like a pro, change things on your website and make the checkout process easier, and you'll see a huge jump in sales.

Page Analytics, Bounce and Exit Rates: Find the pages that get a lot of traffic and make them work better for you. Find out why people are leaving or moving off of pages too quickly if you want to keep them there.

Increasing Average Order Value (AOV): Have you ever thought about how to get people to buy a little more? Upselling, cross-selling, and bundling are all ways to get people to spend more on each deal.

Optimizing your entry pages: These are the first things people see when they visit your site. Make them shine to get more people to buy them. To find the best layout, headlines, and text, try out a few different ones.

Look at your traffic sources to see where your sales are coming from. Distribute resources based on which routes work best. Focus on what brings in the most money, whether it's your marketing budget or your time.

Review and recommendations are your best friends when it comes to customer feedback and social proof. Judge.me and other tools like it help you get and show off good feedback, which builds trust and loyalty. Your best advertising comes from happy customers.

Real-time customer service: For quick help with customers, add live chat tools like Tidio, Shopify Inbox, or Gorgias. Responding quickly shows that you care about your customers and build trust.

Keep in mind that e-commerce is a dynamic field that is always changing. Use podcasts, books, videos, and mentoring to stay up to date on changes in your field. You can change and stay ahead of the curve better if you learn more.

Also, remember this important rule: your people come first. Make sure they're happy, content, and interested. Always keep your customers in mind when you're coming up with new products, making choices, or coming up with new ideas. Customers who are happy will buy from you again, and return customers are what make an online store successful.

Keep your interest alive, stay curious, and be ready to change as you go along this e-commerce path. You're not just starting a business when you put the customer first and work to make things better all the time. You're building a brand that stands out in the vast digital world.

The First Thirty Days of Your Online Business Journey

In order to assist you and guarantee that you set up your store appropriately from the beginning, exactly like the professionals, this step-by-step guide will provide you with assistance and ensure that you follow the professional method. You will be able to have the peace of mind that comes with knowing that you are devoting your time to things that will increase your money and provide you more time for yourself.

There are a number of things that can be performed, including attracting the appropriate clients, gathering the appropriate information, and the subsequent transformation of those clients into delighted customers. At that point, you will be able to keep their company, which will enable you to expand your online business enterprise.

The development of online stores is accomplished through the utilization of this step-by-step approach, which employs a straightforward foundation that is applicable to any online business. By utilizing this strategy, you will be able to ascertain which areas of your online business are in need of development, which duties you need to finish, and how you may complete these jobs in a manner that is both quick and easy.

Attract

Retain

Aquire

Convert

Week 1:

During the initial week following the launch of your website, you should prioritize the verification of component functionality to ensure optimal performance. The process is analogous to verifying the precise alignment of every mechanism in a machine. To achieve this objective, it will be necessary to solicit feedback from others through the means of having them visit your website and offer their input. Their feedback is analogous to having an extra set of eyes examine the work in order to detect any potential errors that may need to be corrected.

However, ensuring proper functionality of everything does not encompass the entirety of the tasks that must be completed. By means of this procedure, you are concurrently implementing a system to track the users who access your website. Consider a scenario in which you are tasked with selecting guests for a gathering. You will have the ability to contact them in the future, potentially to provide them with updates or exclusive promotions. It is comparable to establishing connections and keeping the door open for potential future interactions. In this first week, it is not sufficient to merely initiate activities; rather, preparations must be made for all of the conversations and relationships that will occur in the subsequent weeks.

We aim to accomplish several significant objectives by the end of the week, and they are as follows:

Desktop computers and mobile devices are compatible: Regardless of whether a client is utilizing a desktop computer or a mobile device, your online store must be intuitive and mobile-friendly. This is comparable to maintaining a storefront entrance that is consistently accessible and cordial towards all patrons.

Maintaining a social media presence signifies that you have invested time and energy into immersing yourself in the realm of social media. Comparable to participating in a community where you can engage in dialogue with potential clients and share insights on emerging trends.

The monitoring system has been successfully integrated, providing your shop with a means to observe and record activities. It is analogous to employing an assistant who operates inconspicuously, aiding in the comprehension of client interactions with your establishment and ensuring that all operations run smoothly.

Immediately Usable Marketing Tools: You have taken all the requisite measures to inform the general public about your establishment. A comprehensive assortment of instruments that is ready to tackle a substantial endeavor is comparable to this.

Disseminate News: You have spread the word about your shop to your family and friends, as well as informed them about it. By doing so, you are essentially fostering a sense of community and encouraging others to join in the excitement surrounding your new endeavor.

Therefore, by the conclusion of the week, accomplishing tasks is no longer sufficient; instead, you will have laid the foundation for the subsequent phases of your thrilling expedition.

Attract

Website Wonder:

Ensure your website is a true marvel by making it work seamlessly on both mobile devices and desktop computers. Think of it as creating a grand entrance for visitors, ensuring they have a delightful experience, no matter how they choose to explore your digital haven.

Social Media Spectacle:

Picture this: Your shop is like a dazzling show, and Facebook, Instagram, and TikTok are vibrant stages where you can showcase your unique offerings. It's time to set up accounts on these platforms and let the world witness the magic you're bringing to the digital stage.

Insights Unleashed with Google Analytics:

Now, imagine having a secret guide to the backstage of your online spectacle. Google Analytics is your backstage pass, revealing where your audience is most captivated. It's like peering into the minds of your digital visitors, understanding their preferences, and tailoring your performance for maximum impact.

Golden Invitations:

As the curtains rise, you want your closest allies to witness the grand premiere. Crafting an email is like sending out golden invitations, each containing a virtual treasure map leading your friends and family straight to your digital storefront. It's an open call for them to revel in the wonders you've curated in your online sanctuary.

Buckle up, visionary. Your digital expedition is about to unfold, and the world is eagerly awaiting the showcase of your digital brilliance.

Aquire

Digital Spark:

Imagine adding a dash of magic to your website with the Meta Pixel. It's like unlocking a secret chamber of insights, helping you understand your visitors' moves. And creating a Meta Ad Account? That's your golden ticket to spellbinding promotions that captivate your audience.

Navigating with Google's Map:

Think of your website as a treasure island, and Google as your trusted navigator. Handing over your sitemap.xml is like giving them a well-drawn map, ensuring every nook and cranny of your digital treasure trove is discovered.

Crafting the Social Symphony:

Now, picture your social media as a stage, and each post you make is a note in a captivating symphony. Posting once or twice a day is like composing a melody that keeps your audience humming along. And those hashtags? They're like the magic dust that makes your posts stand out in the vast social galaxy.

Feel the sparks igniting, the anticipation building? Your digital saga is on the verge of unfolding, promising a tale of legendary proportions.

Convert

Showcase on Facebook:

Ever thought of putting your amazing products in front of countless potential buyers? Well, connect your Product Catalog to Facebook, and voila. It's like turning on the spotlight for your treasures.

Google Ads:

Imagine your products starring in a digital blockbuster. To make it happen, set up your Google Ads account. It's like reserving front-row seats for your products in the vast online theater.

Google Merchant Center:

Ready to unveil your offerings to the world? Set up your Google Merchant Center account, it's your backstage pass to ensure your products shine on the grand e-commerce stage.

These steps? Consider them your secret recipe for turning your products into the stars of the show. Let's make your sales story unforgettable.

Retain

Email Marketing Mastery:

Ever dreamed of having a direct line to your customers, keeping them in the loop about your fantastic deals and news? Well, it's time to set up an account with an email marketing wizard like Klaviyo or Mailchimp. Think of it as having a trusty messenger to spread the word about your shop's awesomeness.

Discounts that Sparkle:

Picture this: Your website becomes a treasure trove, and to access the treasures, visitors just need to share their email. Create a tempting discount sign-up—kind of like a magical door that opens to exclusive deals. It's the secret handshake to welcome new customers into your fantastic world.

The Power of Personalized Connection:

Your email list is not just a collection of addresses; it's a community of engaged souls. With each message, you're forging a personal connection, making your customers feel like VIPs with insider access to your world.

Setting up your email marketing platform and enticing visitors with exclusive deals does more than just develop your email list; it creates a world where every communication is a chapter in your brand's story. Prepare to be enchanted and captivated.

WEEK 2:

Ever dreamt of telling the world about your fantastic business? Week 2 is all about making some noise, letting everyone know you're here to bring something special to the table. It's like inviting people to a party and making sure they remember the invite.

Now, let's talk about a cool concept called "working the funnel." Imagine a funnel where you pour in curious folks at the top. That's what we're doing, grabbing attention, getting people interested in your brand.

Think of making an ad like putting up a cool sign on a busy street. It's your way of saying, "Hey, check out what we've got" Once they're intrigued, we'll guide them to your website, like capturing the interest you've stirred up.

Dive into community groups on social media; it's like mingling at a friendly neighborhood gathering. Share your thoughts, let people know you are part of the community.

Write a blog on your website, think of it as sharing your story with friends. And don't keep it to yourself, share it on your other social platforms. It's like spreading the news about a great story you want everyone to know.

Now, let's prep for the "bottom of the funnel", the part where visitors become customers. How? By offering them something special, like a VIP pass to your shop. It's the incentive that says, "Come on back, we've got something you'll love."

Ever wished you had a magical helper? That's where automated marketing comes in. It's like having a trusty sidekick that keeps the excitement alive, even when you're not actively working on it.

Get ready for the grand show, where every step is a move towards making your brand the talk of the town.

Attract

Tell Your Story:

Have you ever considered putting your ideas out there? Now is the perfect moment to post your first blog entry. Imagine that you are sending a letter to your friends, and we will make sure that everyone receives a copy by posting it on your social media accounts.

Join the Neighborhood:

Imagine your business is a cozy house in a friendly neighborhood. Joining Facebook groups and other communities in your niche is like getting to know your neighbors. It's a chance to share tips, learn, and maybe even make some lifelong friends.

Spy on Success:

You may view what's occurring on your website behind closed doors by using Google Analytics. It's similar to monitoring foot traffic in your store on a daily basis to see what draws customers in and how to make your space even more engaging.

Are you prepared to walk onstage and leave your imprint now? Together, we can make your company the talk of the town.

Aquire

Shine Bright on Social:

Ever dreamt of seeing your brand sparkle on Facebook and Instagram? It's time to create a Brand Ad, think of it as a dazzling showcase where your business steals the spotlight and leaves everyone wanting more.

Unlock the Power of Emails:

Picture this: Your brand is like a treasure chest, and email addresses are the golden keys to unlock its secrets. Create a 'Lead Generation' ad on Facebook, offering the same awesome deal as on your website. It's like inviting everyone to join an exclusive club with VIP access to your best offers.

Get ready to make waves in the digital ocean. Your brand is about to become the talk of the town.

Convert

Win Them Over Again:

Ever wished you could bring back visitors who checked out your shop but didn't quite make it to the checkout? Set up a retargeting campaign, it's like extending a warm invitation for a second chance, sweetened with a tempting 20% offer. Imagine it as your shop giving them a friendly nudge to come back and grab what they missed.

Rule Google's Kingdom:

Now, let's conquer the vast digital realm with a Google PMAX campaign. Think of it as planting your flag on the digital map, ensuring your shop is the go-to destination when people are looking for what you offer. It's like setting up a grand billboard on the internet highway, making your brand unmissable.

Get ready to turn those clicks into customers and make your brand a digital sensation.

Retain

Rescue Those Abandoned Carts:

Ever feel that pang of regret when you leave items in your online cart? Imagine giving your customers a friendly nudge to come back and complete their purchase. Set up a Cart Abandonment Email Flow, it's like sending a digital lifeline, saying, "Hey, your items miss you, and here's a little something to sweeten the deal.

Roll Out the Red Carpet for Newbies:

Picture this: A new customer steps into your virtual store. Welcome them like a cherished guest with an email welcome series. It's like a warm handshake and a personal tour, making them feel right at home.

Gratitude in Every Pixel:

Every purchase is a celebration, right? Show your gratitude with a Thank You Email. It's like sending a heartfelt thank-you card, making your customers feel appreciated for choosing your brand.

These email tricks aren't just about messages; they're about building a connection that keeps customers coming back for more. Get ready to turn your shoppers into devoted fans.

Week 3:

Week 3 is your chance to spread the word far and wide. Think of it like planting seeds of curiosity both online and offline. It's not just about reaching more people; it's about opening new doors to opportunities that will keep your brand buzzing.

Now, let's delve into the 'mid-funnel', an exciting phase where extended paid advertising takes center stage. Imagine it like a spotlight, keeping your brand shining in the digital arena. And here's a golden tip: Start listening to what real people are saying about your store. It's like having a backstage pass to tweak and tune your shop to perfection.

This week isn't just about outreach; it's about creating a symphony of success that resonates with your audience. Get ready to amplify your brand's melody.

Picture this: Your brand is like a rocket, and this week, we're launching it into the vast realms of Google and Facebook. It's not just about ads; it's about creating a magnetic pull that draws in new fans and customers.

Ever had that feeling of finding a surprise gift? Let's remind your existing customers that there's a special offer waiting just for them. It's like sending a little love note saying, "Hey, we've got something awesome with your name on it."

Time to turn your customers into advisors. Imagine sitting down for a chat with them, learning about their thoughts and experiences. It's like having a secret weapon, real insights from real people to shape your brand.

Your brand is about to take the stage. Let's put together a plan that's like choreographing a dance of promotions. It's not just about selling; it's about creating an experience that your customers won't want to miss.

Ever wondered why some items fly off the shelf while others linger? Let's look for clues, insights that tell us what makes your customers click that 'Buy Now' button.

Email addresses are like golden tickets to your brand's VIP party. Let's add more names to your guest list. Imagine it as making sure every interested person gets a special invite to the coolest party in town.

This week isn't just about tasks; it's about orchestrating a symphony of success that leaves your audience cheering for an encore. Get ready to make waves.

Attract

Share Your Story Again:
Remember that awesome feeling when you shared your first story? Let's do it again. Publish your second blog post and spread the word on your social media. It's like writing another chapter of your brand's adventure, and this time, it's going to be even more captivating.

Team Up with Influencers:
Ever dreamt of having some cool, influential friends who love your stuff? Reach out to influencers, they're like the rockstars of the online world. Imagine them wearing your brand and singing its praises. It's not just promotion; it's creating a fanbase that trusts and loves your products.

Beyond the Digital Horizon:
Online is fantastic, but let's not forget the real world. Explore 'offline' marketing options, it's like stepping out from behind the screen and introducing your brand to people in your community. Think of it as hosting a fabulous neighborhood party where everyone is talking about your amazing products.

Aquire

Mirror the Magic with Meta:

Imagine doubling the magic of your brand. Create a look-alike Meta brand ad, it's like finding a twin for your brand, doubling the charm, and attracting a whole new set of fans.

Win Hearts with a Contest:

Have you ever contemplated planning a social gathering in which each participant is guaranteed a chance to win? Initiate a competition by organizing a celebratory occasion and Motivating Attendees to Engage. Nevertheless, the pivotal element is that participants can acquire entry by securing a ticket with their email address in exchange for admittance. This occasion transcends being a mere competition and instead fosters the formation of a community comprised of fervent participants.

Craft Your Sales Symphony:

Your brand is about to take center stage. Fill out your Six Week Sales Plan, it's like composing a melody that resonates with your audience. Every note is a step towards making your brand the talk of the town.

Convert

Friendly Nudge for Discount Lovers:

Have you ever left a party without your bag of treats? Allow us to save your guests from missing out. Please remind discount-registered users by email. Like a friendly reminder, it says, "Hello, your exclusive offer is ready for you."

Facebook Magic for Window Shoppers:

Imagine your merchandise winking at customers after they leave. Facebook catalog retargeting ads are like digital signs that say, "You liked these. Still waiting for you."

Fixing Leaks in Your Digital Ship:

Leaky faucets drip water. Let's check your digital leakage. Google Analytics' 'Bounce rates' and departure rates are like ship holes to mend. We want your guests to stay, not go.

Retain

Chat Live, Thrive Live:
Ever wish you could have a friendly chat with your favorite store? Now you can be that awesome shop. Set up Live Chat or Messenger to chat directly with your customers. It's like having a personal shopping assistant right at their fingertips, making their experience feel special and unique.

FAQs that Speak Your Customer's Language:
Think of your FAQs as a guidebook for your brand. Update it with any feedback you've received, it's like adding new chapters based on what your customers are curious about. This way, your customers can find answers easily, making their journey with your brand smoother and more enjoyable.

Turn Customers into Stars:
Imagine your customers sharing their experiences like rock stars. Set up a product review platform, like Judge.me, it's like creating a stage for your customers to shine. Their reviews become the stars of the show, guiding new shoppers and building trust in your brand.

Week 4:

Week 4 is your chance to make your site even more awesome based on what your customers are saying. Think of it like upgrading your favorite hangout spot to make it cozier and more enjoyable. It's not just about what you like; it's about what they love.

Imagine your sales as a rhythmic dance, and Week 4 is when the music starts playing. Send your first campaign email, it's like sending out the invitations to your sales party. Let's also set up a 'split test'—it's like trying out different dance moves to see which one the crowd loves.

Your ads are like the performers on stage. Let's optimize the show, kill the ones that aren't getting applause. It's not about quantity; it's about quality, making sure every ad is a superstar.

Your products are the main stars. Ensure they're showcased correctly on your site, it's like arranging a shop window to make every item look irresistible. Imagine walking by and thinking, "I need that."

This week isn't just about actions; it's about orchestrating a symphony that makes your site a favorite destination and your sales a dazzling performance. Get ready to shine.

Attract

Tell Your Story Again:

It's time to add another exciting chapter to your brand's story. Publish your third blog post and let the world know about it by sharing it on your social playground. Think of it as writing a letter to friends, sharing what's new and exciting.

Team Up for Success:

Ever dreamt of having powerful allies on your journey? Reach out to potential companies for partnerships. It's like building a superhero team, combining strengths for a powerful impact. Together, you can achieve more than you could alone.

Turn Fans into Creators:

Imagine your customers not just loving your brand but also creating content for it. Connect with content creators to get User-Generated Content (UGC). It's like turning your fans into stars, showcasing their experiences and making your brand even more relatable.

Aquire

Brand Magic Unleashed:

Ever thought of making your brand ads even more captivating? Now's the time. Review, optimize, and scale them. It's like polishing the gems of your brand, making sure they shine brighter and attract more admirers.

Inbox Symphony Begins:

Picture this: Your first email marketing campaign is like sending out invitations to a grand celebration. It's not just an email; it's the opening note of a symphony aligned with your 'Six Week Sales Plan.' Get ready to make your audience dance to your brand's rhythm.

This isn't just about tasks; it's about creating experiences that leave a lasting impression. Get ready to witness your brand steal the show.

Convert

Upgrade with Google Magic:

Imagine adding a touch of magic to your website. Install Google Optimize; it's like giving your site a superhero suit. Run your first split test using findings from Google Analytics, it's not just about making changes; it's about making your site even more powerful based on what your audience loves.

Spotlight on Best Sellers:

Your best-selling products are like the stars of your show. Merchandise them on your site; it's like putting them in the front row, making sure they grab all the attention. Imagine your shop as a stage, and these products are the headliners.

Craft Perfect Product Pages:

Think of your product pages as the red carpet for your items. Ensure all products are enriched using 'The Perfect Product Page' guide; it's like giving each item a glamorous makeover. It's not just about selling; it's about creating an experience that leaves your customers saying, "I need this."

Retain

Customer Cheers, Personally:

Imagine your customers as friends at a gathering. Reach out personally to ask about their experience, it's like mingling at a party, hearing their thoughts, and making sure they feel valued. It's not just about feedback; it's about building relationships.

Retain with heartfelt emails:

Your customers are like cherished guests; let's keep them coming back for more. Set up retention email marketing flows; it's like sending them love notes, reminding them why your brand is special. Look for outsourcing and automation opportunities, it's not just about saving time; it's about ensuring every message feels personal and heartfelt.

This isn't just about tasks; it's about creating connections that turn customers into loyal fans. Get ready to elevate your brand's relationship with those who matter most.

Unlock Ecommerce Secrets with Bonus Tips

Ready to dive into the exciting world of ecommerce? Here's your bonus tips:

Bonus Tip 1: Making A Logo

Heare are some great websites to start designing your business logos.

Fiverr (fiverr.com):

- Fiverr is a popular freelance marketplace where you can find graphic designers offering logo design services.
- Features:
    - Access to a diverse pool of freelancers worldwide.
    - Offers various pricing packages to suit different budgets.
    - Ability to view portfolios and reviews of designers.
    - Simple and user-friendly platform.

Upwork (upwork.com):

- Upwork is a global freelancing platform that connects businesses with freelancers, including logo designers.
- Features:
    - Large pool of skilled designers from around the world.
    - Provides options for hourly or project-based work.
    - Offers collaboration tools and project tracking.
    - Secure payment and dispute resolution features

Freelancer (freelancer.com):

- Freelancer is a platform that connects businesses with freelancers across various fields, including graphic design for logos.

- Features:

    o Competitive bidding system for projects.

    o Escrow payment system for secure transactions

    o Extensive talent pool with diverse skill sets.

    o Real-time chat and project collaboration tools.

DesignEvo (designevo.com):

- DesignEvo is an online logo-making tool that allows users to create custom logos using pre-designed templates.

- Features:

    o DIY platform for creating logos without hiring a designer.

    o Extensive library of templates and icons.

    o User-friendly interface with drag-and-drop functionality.

    o Affordable pricing for high-resolution logo downloads

When choosing a platform, consider your budget, design preferences, and whether you want to work directly with a designer or use a DIY tool. Each platform has its strengths, so exploring their features and user reviews can help you make an informed decision based on your specific logo design needs.

Bonus Tip 2: Optimizing Shopify Product Pages for Skyrocketing Sales

Ready to turn your Shopify store into a sales powerhouse? Let's make your online shop not just a place to browse but a destination where sales thrive.

Harness the Power of Conversion Signals: Ever wondered how to push potential customers from 'thinking about it' to 'must-have'? We'll spill the beans on conversion signals, elements like customer reviews, limited-time offers, and low stock alerts. These cues create urgency, nudging visitors to hit that 'Buy Now' button.

Remove Purchase Hurdles with Risk Removal Tactics: Let's erase doubts and hesitation. Money-back guarantees, free shipping, and easy returns become your superheroes. By removing the risk, you're inviting customers to shop with confidence.

Craft Compelling Copy and Build Trust: Words matter. Your product page copy should be a persuasive storyteller, clear, concise, and compelling. Address customer concerns and showcase benefits. And trust elements? Think security badges and customer reviews, they're your credibility boosters.

Design a Visual Feast for Your Customers: First impressions count. Create visually stunning and user-friendly product pages. Mobile optimization is a must, let's make sure your customers have a seamless shopping experience, whether on a phone, tablet, or desktop.

Create Your Sales Masterpiece: Your product page should be a masterpiece. From clear call-to-action buttons to a layout that keeps customers hooked.

Bonus Tip 3: Unlock More Sales Without Spending Too Much on Ads

Ready to boost your sales without breaking the bank on ads? This is your tip to increasing revenue without reaching for your wallet. Let's dive into strategies that'll have customers knocking on your digital door.

Okay, let's keep it simple. Traffic is the heartbeat of your store, it's what brings people in, setting the stage for sales and scaling your e-commerce empire. Now, imagine traffic as a trio, categorized into three key areas:

Sponsored Traffic Examples: Google Ads, Meta (Facebook) ads, TikTok Ads, Pinterest Ads, Spotify ads, Bing ads, affiliate marketing, paid influencers, and paid media. It's like the VIP section, pay to play and get noticed.

Held Traffic: This is your personal treasure trove of data, email, SMS, customers list, pixel data, social followers, YouTube channel, blogs, Facebook groups, and other social media channels. You own it, you control it, and you market it.

Acquired Traffic: You've got to earn it. SEO, 3rd party blog posts, back links, brand reviews, cross promotions, word of mouth, referrals, reviews, social proof, and collaborations It's the street cred you build by actively attracting visitors.

Here's the deal, relying solely on one traffic source is a bit like putting all your eggs in a precarious basket. If that basket breaks, so does your business. Imagine this: You're an e-commerce wizard, and your only trick is sponsored ads. They're working like magic until one day they start misbehaving. Budgets skyrocket, traffic drops, and sales take a nosedive. Why? Because you put all your energy into one source that you decided to play hard to get.

Why One Traffic Source is a No-Go:

Think of it like a tightrope walk without a safety net. If your sole reliance is on sponsored ads, you're gambling. What if the platform changes or competition heats up? Your traffic may vanish faster than a magician's disappearing act.

Here's the game plan. Different traffic sources have different speeds. Some sprint, some stroll. By embracing held, acquired, and sponsored, you're building a fortress for your e-commerce kingdom. It's about not putting all your eggs in one basket but having a diversified portfolio that can weather any storm.

The Result = Ecommerce Triumph

Picture this: your store is a powerhouse. You're not just relying on sponsored ads; you're working the SEO game, crafting emails, engaging with the media, rocking social media, growing that email list, teaming up with brands, collaborating with influencers, and testing ads. It's the ultimate traffic symphony, and the result? Consistent sales, growing brand awareness, and a money-making machine in the making.

So, here's the takeaway: Diversify, conquer, and watch your e-commerce empire thrive. Don't just dream of success; make it a reality.

Bonus Tip 4: Unleash the Power of SMS

Let's also dive into a game-changer you might be underestimating. SMS messages for your brand. I get it; sending texts might seem daunting, especially if you're not a fan of receiving them yourself. But trust me, this is a game you don't want to sit out.

Let's face it, emails are flooding inboxes every day, and they often get lost in the shuffle. Enter SMS, the superhero that cuts through the noise. These messages have a higher chance of being read and clicked because they create a personal connection with your customers.

Picture this: Instead of bombarding your customers with automated emails, imagine having a cozy 1-on-1 chat with them. That's the magic of SMS, it feels personal, relevant, and downright valuable.

If you're sticking to automated emails alone, it's time to shake things up. Incorporate SMS into your flows, especially in welcome, abandon cart, and thank you messages. It's not about spam; it's about delivering content that your customers actually find useful.

Want to hit the conversion jackpot? Personalize your messages. A warm welcome, a gentle nudge about abandoned carts, and a heartfelt thank you after a purchase, SMS lets you add that personal touch that makes all the difference.

Worried about bombarding customers? Don't be. It's about delivering timely and valuable content that enhances their shopping experience. The real trick is understanding your customers, segment them based on preferences and behaviors, and tailor your SMS accordingly.

Turn your SMS messages into a conversation. It's not about broadcasting marketing noise; it's about engaging, providing value, and building a relationship with your customers.

Let's elevate your e-commerce game together. Embrace the power of personalized, relevant messaging, and watch those conversions skyrocket.

Bonus Tip 5: Turn One-Time Shoppers into Lifelong Fans

We all know snagging that first sale is like landing a date, it takes effort. But what comes after that first purchase is equally crucial, yet often overlooked. Picture it as dating in the e-commerce world.

You've successfully landed that date or made that sale. Now, to score a second date or keep customers coming back, you need to stay top-of-mind and keep the spark alive.

Step 1: Create Unforgettable Experiences

Thank-you messages: Start with a heartfelt thank you to show appreciation.

Delivery Updates: Keep the excitement alive with timely delivery updates.

Dispatch: Aim to beat your dispatch times; surprise them with an early package.

Enhance the 'In-Parcel' Experience

Surprise Gift: Include a little extra something for that wow factor.

Personal Note: A handwritten thank-you note for a human touch.

Unique Packaging: Invest in branded packaging for an Instagram-worthy moment.

Bounce Back Offer: Slip in a coupon for their next purchase.

Share and Win: Encourage social media sharing with a special hashtag.

Step 2: Persuade to Come Back

Replenishment: Offer a convenient replenishment program for consumables.

Associated Products: Suggest related products based on their first purchase.

New Products: Showcase your latest arrivals to keep them curious.

Step 3: Reward Loyalty

Spend and Save: Offer discounts for specific spending thresholds.

Earn Points: Implement a points system for every purchase or engagement.

Get Coupons: Send exclusive coupons for anniversaries or milestones.

Step 4: Win Them Back

Price Drops: Notify them when the price drops on a product they view.

Secret Offers: Send exclusive offers to dormant customers.

Invite-Only Events: Host special events or sales exclusively for past customers.

Remember, it's not just about revenue; it's about building lasting relationships. When you create memorable experiences and implement incentive programs, you're not just selling products, you're selling an unforgettable journey your brand can provide. Let's turn those one-time shoppers into lifelong fans.

Bonus Tip 6: Unlock the Power of Your Email List

Picture this: your email list isn't just a mundane collection of names; it's a vibrant community eagerly anticipating every update from your brand. They thrive on your content, love what you stand for, and can't get enough of your offerings. But the burning question is, where do you find these enthusiastic souls?

Well, worry not. This book is your roadmap to discovering these gems and implementing irresistible strategies that will send your email list soaring to new heights.

Discounts: Who doesn't love a good deal? Serve up an unbeatable discount to capture attention and secure your place in their inbox. It's a win-win.

Competitions: Launch a competition and watch people flock to join your email list for a chance to win. It's the golden ticket to winning them over.

VIP Treatment: Offer exclusive access, deals, and events to make subscribers feel like VIPs. It breeds loyalty, and they get the special treatment they crave.

Unlocking the Vault of Information: The opportunities for capturing data are endless. It's not just about name and email anymore. Premium incentives deserve premium information, leading to enhanced personalization and, in turn, more loyalty.

On Your Website: Your site is your virtual playground. Use pop-ups, flyouts, and app notifications to capture data. Optimize for mobile and desktop, and don't forget the on-exit discount pop-up.

At Checkout: The checkout page is your final frontier. Slide in some persuasive copy to encourage visitors to join the email train before sealing the deal.

Ads: Facebook lead ads and Google Ads sitelinks are the sneaky ninjas of email capture. They let users join your list without interrupting their online adventures.

Multi-Channel: Don't limit yourself to one platform. Shout your incentives from the virtual rooftops through social media, posts, Facebook groups, and blog posts. Make them impossible to ignore.

With these strategies in place, you'll become the email list king, utilizing every effective method to create urgency and value. Make them feel like they're missing out by not being part of your email list.

So, there you have it, folks, the playbook to growing your email list with every effective strategy in the book. Implement these, and you'll witness your email list explode with people eager to be a part of your world and enjoy all the benefits that come with it. Are you ready to take your email game to the next level? Let's do this.

Bonus Tip 7: Chat GPT Prompts in Ecommerce

Chat GPT Website: https://chat.openai.com/

Product Descriptions Example 1:

Prompt 1: Pretend to be an online store that sells [what you sell in your store]. Do you get it?

Prompt 2: Write an online product description for [insert product name] that will get a lot of sales. With the following features [list of traits]. The product is meant to be used by [an avatar of the product] and for [the goal of the product].

Note: The summary should have an introduction paragraph, a list of five bullet points that explain the benefits of the features, and then a paragraph that says who the product is for and how it should be used.

Prompt 3: Write the product description in HTML code.

Prompt 4: Write a 150-character meta description for the item.

Product Descriptions Example 2:

Prompt 1: Pretend you are an online store that sells [what does your store sell]; do you get it?

Prompt 2: The person who needs this product is having trouble with [the problem your product fixes]. Your tool is what they need to fix this issue. They will have a bad feeling if they don't get this thing. These features [insert list of features] will make the trouble go away in [your product]. It will make them feel good if they buy this product. Get it?

Prompt 3: Write an e-commerce product description for the product that is focused on making sales. The format should be: first, a line that says what problem the product solves. Then, there is a paragraph that says how the product solves the problem. Next, use the product's features to come up with five perks. Write them down in bullet points. The last thing you should say is how they'll feel if they buy the goods now that the problem has been fixed.

Prompt 4: Write the product description in HTML code

Prompt 5: Write a 150-character meta description for the item.

Collection Descriptions Example:

Prompt 1: Pretend you are an online store that sells [what does your store sell]; do you get it?

Prompt 2: Write a 400-word description of a collection of products in the category [name of collection] that includes the following types of products [insert product types]. Use the following keywords [insert at least 5 SEO keywords] as much as possible in your description."

Tip: The Google Keyword Planner can help you find terms.

Prompt 3: Write the product description in HTML code

Prompt 4: Write a 150-character meta description for the item.

Blogs Writing Example:

Prompt 1: Pretend you are an online store that sells [what does your store sell]; do you get it?

Prompt 2: Come up with five catchy blog post names for the keyword phrase [your blog idea].

Prompt 3: From now on, everything should be written in [your language]. Do you get it?

Prompt 4: Write a 1,000-word blog post about your idea [blog title idea] and include these five keywords in the post [your keywords].

Prompt 5: Write a 150-character meta description for the item.

Bonus Tip 8: Recommended Shopify Apps

- Bulk Discount and Sales Manager

- Sticky Cart by Qikify

- Free Shipping Bar

- Frequently Bought Together

- Multi-Currency

- TinyIMG SEO & Speed

- Goaffpro – Affiliate Marketing

- PageFly Page Builder

- Klaviyo

- Printful: Print on Demand

- Zipify One Click Upsell

- Retarget App

- NoFraud

- BIG Digital Download

- SMS Bump Marketing and Automation

- Marketplace Connect

- Kiwi Size Chart

- Avada Trust Badges Sale Pop-up

- DSers – AliExpress Dropshipping

- Avada SEO Suite

- Push Owl

- Order Metrics

- TimexBar Stock Countdown Timmer

- TrustedSite – Trust Badges

- Privacy & Compliance

- In Card Upsell

- Judge.me Reviews

- Original Wheelio Spin Pop-Ups

- Google & YouTube

- TikTok

- Happy Birthday Email

- Help Center

Bonus Tip 9: Digital Marketing and Ecommerce Terminology

Learn key digital marketing ecommerce terminology. It's like getting a backstage pass to the coolest party in town, where every word is a key to unlock secrets that make your online journey smoother and more thrilling. Don't just be a spectator; be a participant in the digital marketing and ecommerce conversation. Get ready to impress and navigate the digital marketing and ecommerce landscape like a pro.

Let's break down some cool digital marketing terms that might sound a bit techy, but trust me, they're the secret sauce to boosting your online presence:

UGC (User Generated Content): It's like getting your fans to create content for you. Imagine your customers sharing their experiences with your product – that's UGC.

CTA (Call to Action): This is like your digital cheerleader. It's that button or message saying, "Hey, click here!" and leads your audience to take a specific action, like buying your awesome stuff.

EDM (Email Marketing): Think of EDM as your friendly emails that keep your audience in the loop. It's not just about sending emails; it's about building a connection with your peeps.

SEO (Search Engine Optimization): Ever wondered how to get your website to show up on Google? SEO is the magic that helps your site get noticed by the search engines.

SEM (Search Engine Marketing): This is like giving your website a little boost. With SEM, you can run ads on search engines to make sure your brand shines right at the top.

SERP (Search Engine Results Page): Ever googled something and got a bunch of results? That's the SERP – where the magic happens, and you want your website to be right there!

SMM (Social Media Marketing): Think Facebook, Instagram, Twitter – SMM is about being where your audience hangs out. It's like throwing a virtual party for your brand.

Affiliate Marketing: Picture this – you put an ad on another website, and if someone clicks and buys something, you give them a high-five in the form of a commission. Win-win!

Google Index: This is like making sure Google knows you exist. Your web pages get captured, so when someone searches, your site can pop up.

Google Merchant Center: This is Google's way of helping you sell stuff. It's like your virtual marketplace where you showcase your products.

DPA (Dynamic Product Ad): Fancy ads that change based on what your customers like. It's like having a personal shopping assistant for each visitor.

TLA (Text Link Ad): Simple and effective – it's an ad with a clickable text link. Direct and to the point!

Retargeting: Ever visit a website and then suddenly see ads for it everywhere? That's retargeting – reminding those who've shown interest in your brand to come back for more.

Let's chat about some e-commerce secrets that'll make your online store a real winner. Don't worry if these terms sound like a foreign language right now, I'm here to make it all crystal clear.

Traffic: Imagine a bustling street full of people. That's what we call traffic – the number of folks visiting your online store. More traffic means more potential customers!

AOV (Average Order Value): Think of this as the average amount each customer spends in one go. We're talking about boosting that number and making each sale count.

CVR (Conversion Rate): Ever wanted to know how many visitors actually make a purchase? That's where the conversion rate comes in – it's like a high-five for turning window shoppers into buyers.

CRO (Conversion Rate Optimization): Let's make your online store irresistible! CRO is like giving it a makeover to turn more visitors into happy customers. It's all about that sweet spot where everyone hits the buy button.

Bounce Rate: Imagine someone peeking into your store and leaving right away without checking anything out. That's the bounce rate – we want to keep it low and keep people browsing!

Exit Page: Ever wondered where people say "goodbye" to your store? That's the exit page. Let's make sure they leave with a smile and maybe a full shopping cart.

GA (Google Analytics): This is like having a backstage pass to see what's happening on your website. GA helps you understand your visitors better so you can give them exactly what they want.

GTM (Google Tag Manager): Think of GTM as your personal assistant. It helps you organize all those little tools and tags on your site, making everything run smoother.

Pixel: It's like having a detective on your site, but a friendly one. The pixel tracks what people do, what they click, what they like – helping you understand your customers and tailor your store to their needs.

Now, why should you care about all this? Well, these are the keys to unlocking success in the online world. More visitors, higher sales, and a website that people love to explore, that's the dream, right?

So, gear up, my friend, With these digital marketing superpowers and e-commerce secrets in your pocket, you're on the fast track to building an online store that not only looks good but also works like a charm. These terms might sound fancy, but they're the keys to making your brand stand out and connecting with your audience. Let's turn those visitors into loyal customers and make your online business a true success story. Happy selling.